A Business Writing Toolkit For Healthcare Professionals

by

Marco Tan M.D.

FIRST EDITION

ISBN: 978-0-9972624-3-8

Disclaimer:

The content of this book is for general informational purposes only. A professional should make their own professional judgement when applying the information and principles within this book. The author takes no responsibility for the use and application of the information described in this book. References are provided for information purposes only and do not constitute endorsement of any websites or other sources.

Contents

Introduction: A Writer's Toolkit

This book is a toolkit. For you to become proficient with these tools, you must put them into practice. This book explores these tools at a basic level. You can read it cover-to-cover, digest all of the material, and familiarize yourself with each of the tools and when to use them. Alternatively, you can skim through it while keeping in mind the writing task ahead, and pick up the points that catch your eye. In this way, you can use it like a box of tools.

Something to consider about written communication is that it's devoid of the non-verbal cues of face-to-face communication. Effective writing that employs the tools presented in this book can compensate for this.

This book puts many otherwise scattered concepts together and puts them into a package specifically for healthcare professionals. All the examples we will discuss will be from a healthcare professional's perspective.

I've written this book for healthcare professionals who are expanding outside of the realm of a traditional clinical practice. These pursuits include healthcare administration, consulting, and business ventures. As a physician who has also been an author, entrepreneur, and marketer, I've taken such a journey myself. In addition to working as an emergency physician, I've written books on medical documentation and clinical decision making, run a small business, and worked as a medical advisor in the pharmaceutical marketing industry.

Through a combination of experiences, I realized how important writing well is in many different venues. I also saw how little there was in the way of content for systematically teaching healthcare professionals how to write well. This book is a way to transmit some of the fundamental lessons I've learned to you.

What Good Business Writing Can Do For Healthcare Professionals

By business writing, I mean any written, professional communication outside of your immediate clinical duties. Common examples include an email, a printed letter, or a slide presentation.

In the years leading up to the writing of this book, the healthcare industry has evolved to encompass many aspects of business. Good writing is one of the tools we can use to better navigate this new landscape and speak with a clearer, more concise voice. Ultimately, this can allow us to have a greater impact on the healthcare industry.

Business writing skills apply to a wide variety of pursuits both inside and outside of traditional, clinical practice. A few examples include:

- Communicating with vendors for your private practice
- Writing a proposal for an initiative to your hospital leadership
- Making a slide presentation for a new initiative within your healthcare system
- Communicating with non-clinicians for consulting opportunities
- Collaborating with non-clinicians on joint projects
- Writing a CV or resume
- Presenting data to your colleagues

In business settings, you're judged on how well or how poorly you communicate. However, writing well is not a standard part of the training for most healthcare professionals. This lack of training puts healthcare professionals at a disadvantage when communicating with those outside the clinical sphere.

Guidelines for Clear Communication

Below are some fundamental guidelines for writing well to achieve clear communication.

The guidelines we will focus on are:

- Write with your audience in mind
- Write short, simple sentences
- Use concrete details
- Lead with your conclusion

Like any guidelines, these are not absolute rules, but patterns that you should follow most of the time.

Write With Your Audience in Mind

Different audiences have different needs. If you address all audiences the same, you run the risk that your reader will not comprehend your intended message. So be sure to take into account what your anticipated audience likely knows and does not know. If practical, ask about the extent of their knowledge on the topic.

When in doubt, add more information rather than less.

Think about your audience when writing your communications and ask yourself:

- What does this audience already know about what I am writing?
- What are this audience's priorities?
- How will my communication fill in the gaps for them?

Consider the following examples:

- Your description of the med-surg workflow to intensive care nurses will be very different than your description of the same workflow to electronic medical records consultants.
- Your description of how you addressed a patient complaint will be different based on whether you're writing to the site director of your clinic, or the director of public relations of your healthcare system.

In both examples above, each audience has different needs, priorities, and understanding of the context of your situation.

Write Short, Simple Sentences

Short sentences give your reader bite-sized bits of information that they can easily digest.

By contrast run-on sentences force readers to mentally swallow many ideas in a single sentence. When possible make sentences bite-sized chunks with one, focused statement per sentence. If you've written a sentence that contains more than one thought, consider rewriting it into shorter, simpler sentences.

Example:

> We were able to tally the quarterly census for orthopedic clinic for the last 8 quarters, and they showed a quarter by quarter increase in volume, compared to the 2 preceding years.

We have several ideas going on in this sentence. We can break it down into 4 discrete sentences, as shown below:

> We tallied the quarterly census for orthopedic clinic. Our tally included the last 8 quarters. There was a quarter by quarter increase in volume. We compared this census to the preceding 2 years.

Example:

> It is appreciated that you spent the time showing me around the radiology department after my interview, as I know you have a very busy schedule.

This sentence rambles a bit. We can divide this easily into 2 ideas.

It is appreciated that you spent the time to showing me around the radiology department after my interview. I know you have a very busy schedule.

Separating the original sentence into 2 makes it easier to understand. As in the previous example, dividing the original into multiple sentences allows your readers to pause, digest the information, and integrate it into the whole story. This enables your reader to understand more in less time and with less effort. Your communication is thus more effective.

Use Concrete Details Whenever Possible

Using concrete details leads to a clearer picture in the mind of your reader. Your readers will have a harder time following vague conceptualizations of your ideas. Concrete details draw a picture of what you're thinking. With this mental picture, your readers are more likely to agree with your point of view, give it more serious consideration, or at the least gain an understanding of what you're conveying.

You can certainly provide too much detail. To minimize this, stick to those few details that will illustrate your point.

Example:

> I habitually found the state of the emergency department security worrisome.

This is a generality without specific details. The above sentence may serve as a fine introduction to a few details, but it's less effective without those details.

> I habitually found the state of the emergency department security worrisome. The last 2 times I was on duty, after staff pushed the panic button, security took more than 10 minutes to arrive. The security booth was empty for over half the time. This booth is supposed to be continuously occupied by security personnel. On the last shift, a rowdy man came into the entrance off the street. He was swearing and shouting at staff. Security was nowhere to be found.

Using concrete details communicates by illustration.

Example:

> Our nursing salaries need to increase as we are not
> competitive in the current market. We are just not
> offering our nurses enough to encourage them to stay.

As in the above example, this speaks generally without
going into specific details. It may serve as a good
introduction, but by itself is an unsupported argument. It
begs to be supported by further details.

> Our nursing salaries need to increase as we are not
> competitive in the current market. Our recruiters tell me
> that our primary competitors in town pay 15% more and
> have a better retirement fund match. On speaking to 4 of
> the nurses who have left to work at other facilities in the
> past 3 months, 3 out of 4 mentioned better salary as their
> primary reason for leaving.

Lead With Your Conclusion

You can think of this as starting the joke with the punchline. This makes for a poor joke, but makes for good business writing.

Most of the time, in business writing we want to get straight to the point. Afterwards, we follow up with details to prove that point.

Leading with the conclusion gives your audience a point to anchor on. With this anchor, your audience has a framework to understand all of the follow-up points. Leading with your conclusion will also make your writing faster to read.

Example:

Patient volume at both urgent care centers has risen dramatically in the last year. Combined volumes have risen by at least 10% each quarter for the last 4 quarters. This is an improvement from the previous 4 quarters when we saw a total decrease in volume of about 7%. Seemingly following this year's trend, patient satisfaction scores have decreased between 2-3% each quarter for the last 4 quarters as well. Front line staff have been repeatedly requesting an additional LPN and PA be added to the schedule. Revenues from increased volume can certainly support the additional staff, will likely lead to improved patient satisfaction scores, and likely lead to increased revenue generation.

This makes for a pretty good story and flows reasonably well. However, it meanders in getting to the conclusion, rather than letting the details support the conclusion.

Instead, consider if we lead with the conclusion that we need more staff:

> Our urgent care centers need additional staffing, based on the results of the past 4 quarters. Patient volume at both urgent care centers have risen dramatically in the last year by at least 10% each quarter for the last 4 quarters. This is an improvement from the previous 4 quarters when we saw a total decrease in volume of about 7%. Seemingly following this year's trend, patient satisfaction scores have decreased between 2-3% each quarter for the last 4 quarters. Front line staff have been repeatedly requesting an additional LPN and PA be added to the schedule. Revenues from increased volume can certainly support the additional staff, will likely lead to improved patient satisfaction scores, and likely lead to increased revenue generation.

The request for more staff frames the specific points of the argument. After the first sentence of the paragraph, the following facts work together to support the point.

Example:

> I was impressed with the professionalism and friendliness of the staff. The feedback mechanism for improving institutional procedures and protocols are also a major asset to your organization. I see room for tremendous growth with what you are building in your department. However, at this time, I cannot accept your generous offer for a position.

In this case, the writing takes the reader in one direction and then suddenly goes in another direction. The suspense is not helping soften the blow. Consider this alternative, in leading with your conclusion.

> Unfortunately at this time, I cannot accept your generous offer for a position. Please do not take this as a reflection on the work your department has done. I was impressed with the professionalism and friendliness of the staff. The feedback mechanism for improving institutional procedures and protocols are also a major asset to your organization. I see also that you have room for tremendous growth. Perhaps in the future I will join when my situation is different.

Building the rejection up with suspense usually makes it worse. It can also be construed as misleading. Do not mislead. Send clear signals, not mixed signals. Be clear with your communication, even when softening the blow of a rejection.

Formatting Tools

Formatting is how you arrange your ideas on a page.

Good formatting makes your content easier to read.

Occasionally, the solution to making your ideas clearer isn't your word choice, style, or grammar. The solution may be how you arrange your ideas in relation to each other.

Good formatting cannot replace poor word choice, style, or grammar. However, it can be a complementary tool to your other writing tools.

Paragraphs

Separate different ideas into different paragraphs. Even if your paragraph is only one sentence, make it its own paragraph if it is its own, distinct idea. The separation gives your readers a moment to pause, digest what they just read, and prepare themselves for the next thought. Do not risk losing some of your thoughts, or readers, in a jumble of ideas.

Example:

> I am writing to follow-up on our meeting last week for potentially consulting for your medical software company. As a reminder, I have over 10 years of experience on the front line of healthcare in addition to 2 years as a healthcare systems consultant for an up-and-coming medical group in my area. I continue to believe that these experiences would be a valuable asset to your software company as it is getting off of the ground. Please let me know if you would like a follow-up call to discuss how we might proceed.

Even though this is a relatively short paragraph, it contains 3 distinct ideas that we can separate to make this communication clearer and easier to understand for our reader.

> I am writing to follow-up on our meeting last week for potentially consulting for your medical software company.
>
> As a reminder, I have over 10 years of experience on the front line of healthcare, in addition to 2 years as a

healthcare systems consultant for an up-and-coming medical group in my area. I continue to believe that these experiences would be a valuable asset to your software company as it is getting off the ground.

Please let me know if you would like a follow-up call to discuss how we might proceed.

Through using paragraphs, we make the ideas easier to digest and call more attention to each individual idea. In this case, it helps focus the reader on the years of experience, which the writer is leaning on heavily as the key to their value in this potential working relationship.

Example:

In response to the patient complaint about the doctor and nurse on the 20th of April, I completed my investigation of this allegation. My investigation included contacting the patient, the doctor in question, and the nurse in question. In addition, I questioned another nurse who was in the vicinity of the alleged incident as well as one of the janitorial staff who was present at the time. I spoke to all of these parties at length within the past week regarding this allegation. All parties spoken to had different recollections of the alleged incident. The investigation so far leaves us with no clear, consistent narrative across the board. I will bring these finding up at the next committee meeting, which is scheduled for this coming Tuesday.

There is a lot going on in this paragraph. Now we will see it broken up into several paragraphs. Keep in mind that there is more than one way to break up the pieces.

In response to the patient complaint about the doctor and nurse on the 20th of April, I completed my investigation of this allegation. My investigation included contacting the patient, the doctor in question, and the nurse in question. In addition, I questioned another nurse who was in the vicinity of the alleged incident as well as one of the janitorial staff who was present at the time. I spoke to all of these parties at length within the past week regarding this allegation.

All parties spoken to had different recollections of the alleged incident. The investigation so far leaves us with no clear, consistent narrative across the board.

I'll bring these finding up at the next committee meeting, which is scheduled for this Tuesday.

Each paragraph is a discreet idea, and it is easier to understand when they're separated into different paragraphs for the reader to digest.

Spacing

The concept behind spacing is basically the same as when using paragraphs. You separate ideas to make your readers' understanding easier.

Spacing is an effective tool for when you have no sentences. A good example of this is in a CV.

Example:

```
Bachelor of Science
-University of Maryland
-2000-2005
Doctor of Medicine
-University of Southern California
-2005-2009
Internal Medicine Residency
-University of Southern California
-2009-2012
Rheumatology Fellowship
-University of Maryland
-2012-2014
```

Although the above is certainly readable, adding spaces in a thoughtful way can make the document easier to read, and leave a better impression on your reader. In this example, we will put an extra line between the educational stages and use indentation for the institutions and years.

Bachelor of Science
    -University of Maryland
    -2000-2005

Doctor of Medicine
    -University of Southern California
    -2005-2009

Internal Medicine Residency
    -University of Southern California
    -2009-2012

Rheumatology Fellowship
    -University of Maryland
    -2012-2014

Making these small changes with spacing makes the CV much more readable, leaving a better impression on the reader.

Centering

Centering is placing text in the center of the page. This tool is useful in introducing a new section of text. Common examples would be a CV or in a lengthy report. Think of this tool as akin to separating chapters of a book by adding titles to the beginning of each chapter.

Example:

<u>Education</u>

Bachelor of Science
    -University of Maryland
    -2000-2005

Doctor of Medicine
    -University of Southern California
    -2005-2009

<u>Post-Graduate Training</u>

Internal Medicine Residency
    -University of Southern California
    -2009-2012

Rheumatology Fellowship
    -University of Maryland
    -2012-2014

This is readable, keeps the information organized, and separates different pieces of information from each other. However, using centering to differentiate sections makes this even clearer.

<u>Education</u>

Bachelor of Science
-University of Maryland
-2000-2005

Doctor of Medicine
-University of Southern California
-2005-2009

<u>Post-Graduate Training</u>

Internal Medicine Residency
-University of Southern California
-2009-2012

Rheumatology Fellowship
-University of Maryland
-2012-2014

The above makes the distinction between undergraduate-med school and postgraduate training very clear. The break caused by moving from the left to the centered positions gives a strong signal that you are changing topics.

Example:

Primary Care Patient Volume

Patient volume has increased about 3% compared to the previous 12 months. We can probably attribute this to a combination of community outreach, hiring an additional nurse practitioner…

Primary Care Clinic Revenue

Revenue from the primary care clinic has remained stable this year compared to the previous 3 months, despite the increase in patient volume. Factors contributing to this include mainly change in insurance reimbursement, but other contributing factors include…

Even though these sections are reasonably-well differentiated, we can add a little bit more differentiation by centering the section titles.

Primary Care Patient Volume

Patient volume has increased about 3% compared to the previous 12 months. We can probably attribute this to a combination of community outreach, hiring an additional nurse practitioner…

Primary Care Clinic Revenue

Revenue from the primary care clinic has remained stable this year compared to the previous 3 months, despite the increase in patient volume. Factors contributing to this include mainly change in insurance reimbursement, but other contributing factors include…

The change in format signals to the reader that you are shifting the conversation to a different topic. This kind of change helps the reader identify when you're going to change the subject and helps them make a mental shift to prepare for your change in direction.

Columns

Columns are a way of arranging your ideas that can put them in a smaller space. Columns can be a good idea when you have long lists of items and want to save space. They can also be useful when you want to compare and contrast.

Example:

Thank you for your interest in using me as a medical consultant. Below, you will find a list of actions regarding this project that will be included in my hourly billing:

-Review of scientific materials
-Scientific industry meetings
-Assisting with drafts
-Drafting templates
-Reviewing patient records
-Written communication
-Spoken communication
-Working with other vendors
-Communications with colleagues
-Communication with vendors
-Travel for this project >20 miles from my home

This list certainly covers a lot of detail regarding what will be counted towards billable time. However, if you're short on space, and still want to be organized, you can organize this list into columns

Thank you for your interest in using me as a medical consultant. Below, you will find a list of actions regarding this project that will be included in my hourly billing:

-Review of scientific materials   -Spoken communication
-Scientific industry meetings   -Working with other vendors
-Assisting with drafts   -Communications with colleagues
-Drafting templates   -Communication with vendors
-Reviewing patient records   -Travel for this project >20
-Written communication   miles from my home

Example:

Current Fiscal Year for Emergency Dept
20,115 patient visits
25% admission rate
2% transfer rate
7% 30-day return
Previous Fiscal Year for Emergency Dept
19,500 patient visits
27% admission rate
2% transfer rate
6% 30-day return

We can compare numbers in a list like this. However, it becomes more effective to compare and contrast them when they're side-by-side.

Current Fiscal Year for Emergency Dept	**Previous Fiscal Year for for Emergency Dept**
20,115 patient visits	19,500 patient visits
25% admission rate	27% admission rate
2% transfer rate	2% transfer rate
7% 30-day return rate	6% 30-day return rate

Columns allow for a fast, efficient way to compare multiple sets of data.

Bullet Points

Bullet points are small dots in front of items on a list. They call out the items on a list. They organize them into separate, distinct statements.

Bullet points create a point of focus for your reader, signaling that this is a discrete, important idea.

A few points to keep in mind about using bullet points:

- Make the points short, if possible
- Make sure they follow the same structure
- Make each point a discrete one
- Make each point related to the ones surrounding it

When used correctly, bullet points can communicate a lot of information quickly.

Example:

> The following will be discussed in the department-wide meeting next Monday: purchase of new ultrasound, 3rd quarter healthcare associated pneumonia data, revisions to on-call policy, new medical student rotation curriculum.

Putting a list in this format makes it difficult to read. Using bullet points helps make each idea more prominent, brings attention to it, and separates each idea.

> The following will be discussed in the department-wide meeting next Monday:
> - purchase of new ultrasound
> - 3rd quarter healthcare associated pneumonia data
> - Revisions to on-call policy
> - New medical student rotation curriculum

Example:

> The ICU nurses have noticed a deterioration of their working environment over the past 6 months. The primary issues we want addressed by leadership are strict enforcement of nurse to patient ratios, consistent posting of the contact information of the supervising physician, improving consistency of access for new hires into pharmacy, restricting the supply closet so that it is accessible to ICU staff only, and increasing unit clerk coverage during peak hours.

There are several points here that need to be addressed. But they're jumbled together in a run-on sentence. Breaking the individual grievances into bullet points makes each point distinct.

> The ICU nurses have noticed a deterioration of their working environment over the past 6 months. The primary issues we want addressed by leadership are
> - Strict enforcement of nurse to patient ratios
> - Consistent posting of the contact information of the supervising physician
> - Improving consistency of access for new hires into pharmacy
> - Restricting the supply closet so that it is accessible to ICU staff only
> - Increasing unit clerk coverage during peak hours

Framing the information in this way makes it easier to read and harder to miss each individual point.

Font Tools

We are not going to address choice of specific fonts, as this is beyond our current discussion.

What we will discuss are font tools to bring emphasis to specific portions of text.

You can combine some of these font tools. However, be careful in using too many different font tools in the same writing. This can cause distractions.

Using Italics

Use italics if you want to emphasize a specific point or when you want clear separation between bodies of text.

Example:

Risk management emphasized that documentation from each professional should be completed in a timely manner, ideally within 24 hours of the patient encounter.

We can use italics to emphasize the timeframe.

Risk management emphasized that documentation from each professional should be completed in a timely manner, *ideally within 24 hours of the patient encounter*

Example:

I want to address the specific request from the urology clinic's office manager: "We need additional PA coverage throughout the summer, as 2 of our PA's are on temporary leave and expected back in September."

We can use italics to add extra emphasis on the office manager's message.

I want to address the specific request from the urology clinic's office manager: *"We need additional PA coverage throughout the summer, as 2 of our PA's are on temporary leave and expected back in September."*

Example:

> I have spoken to our IT vendor about coordinating with you to integrate the stroke protocols into the existing system. They say that they can implement the changes by Tuesday of next week, but that they will need until that Friday to complete testing for functionality

We can use italics if we want to emphasize what the IT vendor's timeline.

> I have spoken to our IT vendor about coordinating with you to integrate the stroke protocols into the existing system. They say that they can implement the changes *by Tuesday of next week, but that they will need until that Friday to complete testing for functionality*

Underlining

Like italics, use underlining to emphasize specific points or when you want clear separation between bodies of text. Additionally, underlining is also useful for titles or subtitles.

Example:

This retainer for medical consultation services serves as the complete and total agreement between me and your firm.

If we want to emphasize complete and total, we can use underlining.

This retainer for medical consultation services serves as the <u>complete and total agreement</u> between me and your firm.

Example:

Post op length of stay

Post op length of stays have decreased over this quarter compared to the last 4 quarters…

OR complication rates

OR complication rates have decreased this quarter compared to the last 4 quarters….

We can use underlining to emphasize a title to a section of text. Without underlining, the titles for each section can get lost in the overall body of the text. Underlining can help separate sections of text from their surroundings, and announce the topic of the following content.

<u>Post op length of stay</u>

Post op length of stays have decreased over this quarter compared to the last 4 quarters...

<u>OR complication rates</u>

OR complication rates have decreased this quarter comparted to the last 4 quarters....

Bolding

Bolding is yet another tool that you can use to bring emphasis to your writing. You can use bolding to bring extra attention to the most important part of a sentence.

Example:

> I know that our original plan was for me to start on February 1. However, because of the unexpected events that I am sure you are aware of, I will not be able to start until February 15 at the earliest. Please let me know what steps I can take in the meantime to minimize the disruption this may cause.

There is a lot of information in this paragraph. No one piece of information stands out. By bolding, you can bring focus to the key piece of information you want your reader to know. In this case, let's focus on the earliest start date.

> I know that our original plan was for me to start on February 1. However, because of the unexpected events that I am sure you are aware of, I will not be able to start **until February 15 at the earliest**. Please let me know what steps I can take in the meantime to minimize the disruption this may cause.

Example:

> I wanted to remind you all that the last inservices for the new infusion pumps will be tomorrow at both 7AM and 7 PM.

Here we want to emphasize the times of the inservice.

I wanted to remind you all that the last inservices for the new infusion pumps will be tomorrow at **both 7AM and 7 PM.**

Overusing These Tools

Use the above tools sparingly and strategically to get the most effect out of them. If you overuse these tools, they will lose effectiveness. Overuse also runs the risk of annoying your readers.

If you come to the point where you think, "it's all important and should all be emphasized", then do not use any of these tools at all.

If you want to make something easy for the reader to scan, you can prioritize the most important part of the paragraph or sentence, then apply a tool to only that part.

Example:

> **Pediatric clinic volume has decreased by about 6% over the past calendar year.** The previous 3 years to this, **volume had been stable**. I suspect that the **increase in our urgent care capabilities** to expand to pediatric care are a **major part of this trend**. I have asked our practice manager to reach out to the practice manager for urgent care so that we can **coordinate a joint report.** We expect to have the report to you **by the end of the month.**

Almost half of this paragraph is underlined and bolded for emphasis. It has reached the point that these tools are not helpful in emphasizing the key points. You should be selective when using these tools and use them to emphasize only the most important information.

Applying the Tools to Specific Examples

The remainder of this toolkit will examine specific applications of the basic concepts we discussed earlier. We will examine common examples of business writing that a healthcare professional is likely to encounter: the curriculum vitae, the resume, the email, and the slide presentation.

Curriculum Vitae Basics

A Curriculum Vitae (CV) is a comprehensive list of your educational and professional accomplishments. A CV will be an important document in academic or clinical positions.

Typically, a CV will include sections for your education, work experience, awards, publications, and presentations. Often, people will put relevant volunteer experience in a CV.

The order of these sections may differ depending on your preference, but they will all be in your CV.

Place your accomplishments in order of time. This can be either from most distant to most recent or vice versa.

Keep focused on the concept that a CV is an organized, comprehensive list of your experiences.

Starting on the next page, we will apply the concepts for good business writing into the CV of a fictional surgeon.

Example:

John Doe, MD
Johndoemd@johndoemd.com
Cell (123) 456 7890

Work experience:
Anatomy Laboratory Assistant, University of ABC,
August 2007- May 2009
Surgical Resident, University Hospital of ABC, July
2013- June 2018

Educational experience:
Bachelor of Science in Biochemistry, University of ABC,
June 2009
Doctor of Medicine, XYZ Medical College, June 2013

Presentations:
Common Complications for Laparoscopic
Cholecystectomy, Surgical Grand Rounds, December
2013
Suture Basics and Workshop for Medical Students,
Medical Student Lecture Series for Surgical Rotation,
July 2014, August 2014, December 2015
An Uncommon Complication of AAA Repair, Surgical
Grand Rounds, November 2014
Management of Anastomotic Leak After
Esophagectomy, Surgical Grand Rounds, April 2016
Review of Geriatric Trauma Guidelines, Morbidity and
Mortality Conference, May 2016
Review of Surgical Options for Pancreatic Cancer,
January 2017
Endovascular Aneurysm Repair for Abdominal Aortic
Aneurysm, November 2017

Publications:
Geriatric Trauma: A Review, Journal of General Surgery,
co-author, August 2016
A Novel Approach to Endovascular Repair of AAA,
Journal of General Surgery, co-author, January 2018

Awards:
Resident teacher of the year, 2014
Resident teacher of the year 2017

Volunteer Work:
Medical Mission to Panama with Relief Agency, July
2011

To this raw content of the previous 2 pages, we will apply the concepts we discussed in previous sections.

John Doe, MD
Johndoemd@johndoemd.com
Cell (123) 456 7890

Work experience:
Anatomy Laboratory Assistant
- University of ABC
- August 2007- May 2009

Surgical Resident
- University Hospital of ABC
- July 2013- June 2018

Educational experience:
Bachelor of Science in Biochemistry
- University of ABC
- June 2009

Doctor of Medicine
- XYZ Medical College
- June 2013

Presentations:
Common Complications for Laparoscopic Cholecystectomy
- Surgical Grand Rounds
- December 2013

Suture Basics and Workshop for Medical Students
- Medical Student Lecture Series for Surgical Rotation
- July 2014, August 2014, December 2015

An Uncommon Complication of AAA Repair

- Surgical Grand Rounds
- November 2014

Management of Anastomotic Leak After Esophagectomy

- Surgical Grand Rounds
- April 2016

Review of Geriatric Trauma Guidelines

- Morbidity and Mortality Conference
- May 2016

Review of Surgical Options for Pancreatic Cancer

- Surgical Grand Rounds
- January 2017

Endovascular Aneurysm Repair for Abdominal Aortic Aneurysm

- Surgical Grand Rounds
- November 2017

Publications:

Geriatric Trauma: A Review, Journal of General Surgery, co-author, August 2016

A Novel Approach to Endovascular Repair of AAA, Journal of General Surgery, co-author, January 2018

Awards:

Resident teacher of the year, 2014
Resident teacher of the year 2017

Volunteer Work:

Medical Mission to Panama with Relief Agency, July 2011

You can demonstrate the content in more than one way using many of the same principles.

As an alternative, consider this:

<u>**John Doe, MD**</u>

Johndoemd@johndoemd.com, Cell (123) 456 7890

<u>**Work experience:**</u>

Anatomy Laboratory Assistant, University of ABC

August 2007- May 2009

Surgical Resident, University Hospital of ABC

July 2013- June 2018

<u>**Educational experience:**</u>

Bachelor of Science in Biochemistry, University of ABC

June 2009

Doctor of Medicine, XYZ Medical College

June 2013

<u>**Presentations:**</u>

Surgical Grand Rounds: Common Complications for Laparoscopic Cholecystectomy

---

December 2013

Suture Basics and Workshop

July 2014, October 2014, December 2015

An Uncommon Complication of AAA Repair

November 2014

Management of Anastomotic Leak After Esophagectomy

April 2016

Review of Geriatric Trauma Guidelines

May 2016

Review of Surgical Options for Pancreatic Cancer

January 2017

Endovascular Aneurysm Repair for Abdominal Aortic Aneurysms

November 2017

Med Student Lecture Series: Suture Basics and Workshop

July 2014, October 2014, December 2015

Morbidity and Mortality Conference: Review of Geriatric Trauma Guidelines

May 2016

Publications:

Geriatric Trauma: A Review, Journal of General Surgery, co-author

August 2016

A Novel Approach to Endovascular Repair of AAA, Journal of General Surgery, co-author

January 2018

Awards:

Resident teacher of the year

academic year 2014 - 2015

Resident teacher of the year

 academic year 2017 - 2018

Volunteer Work:

Medical Mission to Panama with Relief Agency

July 2011

Resume Basics

A resume is a curated description of your work experience as it relates to the position you're applying for. In contrast to a CV, <u>a resume gives you the opportunity to focus and expound on your most pertinent experiences</u>.

Think of a resume as a carefully-selected sample of your experiences that demonstrate what you're capable of.

A key aspect to a resume is that you're tailoring it to a specific position in a specific organization.

There are a few ways to format a resume. As a guiding principle—keep it organized and keep that organization consistent.

A resume is commonly used outside of clinical or academic settings.

For the following examples, we'll assume that our fictional surgeon from the CV section is applying for a medical director role in a company that makes continuing medical education courses.

Example:

John Doe, MD
Johndoemd@johndoemd.com, Cell (123) 456 7890

Objective:
Experienced physician with ability to clearly communicate complex topics looking to contribute to the field of medical education.

Professional Experience:
Resident Physician, Surgical Residency University of ABC
July 2013 - June 2018
- Created and presented multiple lectures on a wide variety of topics to trainees in surgical residency
- Published in peer-reviewed literature on surgical topics
- Awarded multiple teaching awards for teaching excellence

Attending Physician, Faculty, Surgical Residency
University of ABC   July 2018 - Present
- Created evidence-based guideline for geriatric trauma that were vetted and utilized in a large, multi-hospital, health system
- Member of resident education committee
- Co-authored evidence-based protocol for treatment of sepsis in surgical intensive care
- Lectured at multiple local and regional conferences regarding geriatric trauma and treatment of post-surgical infections
- Reviewed prospective CME material for University

---

of ABC in pre-publishing stage

Educational Experience:
Bachelor of Science in Biochemistry, University of ABC
June 2009

Doctor of Medicine, XYZ Medical College
June 2013

Awards:
Resident teacher of the year
academic year 2014 - 2015

Resident teacher of the year
academic year 2017 – 2018

One thing to note is that the resume describes not only the positions that you've held, but also a brief narrative of the projects that you've worked on. It tries to connect the specific experiences with the objective. In this case, Dr. John Doe is trying to show a CME-making company that he has plenty of relevant experience making medical education content.

Multiple formats for resumes exist. Here's an alternate form of the resume with a somewhat different format.

The version shown on the following page focuses on the interpersonal aspects of the experiences more than the previous version. However, take note of how the skills that John Doe highlights can still be applicable to the position he seeks. This demonstrates how your resume can tell the same general story, but in a different way.

John Doe, MD
Johndoemd@johndoemd.com, Cell (123) 456 7890

Experience:
Attending Physician, Department of Surgery, University of ABC, July 2018 - Present
- Supervise, train, and evaluate surgical residents
- Experience training different levels of trainee in complex, surgical procedures and complicated surgical management
- Coordinate curriculum refinement with fellow faculty
- Created and implemented evidence-based guidelines within large hospital system
- Collaborated with colleagues on official educational material to be published by university

Surgical Resident, University of ABC, July 2013 - June 2018
- Supervised, train, and evaluate medical students and junior surgical residents
- Taught minor, procedural skills to medical students
- Collaborated with colleagues to design, implement, and publish surgical literature
- Prepared and delivered lectures on a wide range of surgical topics

Education:
Doctor of Medicine, XYZ Medical College
June 2013

Bachelor of Science in Biochemistry, University of ABC
June 2009

<u>Awards:</u>
Resident teacher of the year
academic year 2017 – 2018

Resident teacher of the year
academic year 2014 - 2015

Email Basics

Email is a universal communication tool across many industries. A big advantage to email in business is that it leaves an easily-discovered, written record of your communications. With that in mind, write your emails with as much attention to detail as possible.

Use email wisely. Be mindful of what you write and how you write it.

Keep in mind the concepts for clear communication that we discussed earlier:

- Write with your audience in mind
- Write short, simple sentences
- Use concrete details
- Lead with your conclusion

Also keep in mind tools such as formatting and fonts.

Strive to make your emails clear, direct, and easily understood. A common complaint both inside and outside of healthcare is that email messages are unclear, do not get to their point quickly, and are difficult to understand.

Write Your Emails like Short, Cohesive Essays

Strive for them to be focused, well-thought out, and polished. Like any well-done essay, you should proofread any email before you send it.

In general, your business emails should not be brief, one-liners. Although these occasionally have some use, they mostly clutter your inbox and don't add value to your communication.

Choose One, Main Topic Per Email

As a general rule, having multiple topics per email increases the chance that any one of the topics gets forgotten by your reader.

An email with many details on multiple topics makes it harder to read. Readers are less likely to fully understand or respond to emails with multiple topics.

Example:

> Thank you for the time you spent inservicing the nurses in my department on the new catheters. Every nurse I have spoken to has remarked to me how much more comfortable they feel with this equipment now. If possible, I would like to have you come back for a second session next month when we have a group of new nurses starting.
>
> With regards to the hospital-wide meeting to introduce the new, chief nursing officer, please see attached plans for interdepartmental coordination that we will also unveil at that meeting. Hopefully we can get the backing of the new chief nursing officer for this.

This email has 2 subjects and comes across as scattered and unfocused. In this case, each paragraph should be its own email. You may feel like you are doing the reader a favor by combining two messages into one email. Most of the time, you're not. Separate your ideas into different emails to give each idea the attention each it deserves. Doing this increases the chance of the reader addressing both ideas. This minimizes the risk of the reader addressing one message at the expense of another.

The email should contain all the information the recipient should reasonably need

A common mistake is to make an email too cryptic. Your email should clearly state:

- Context for the situation at hand
- Specifics on what you need from the recipient
- What the recipient needs to know in order to take any necessary next steps
- Next steps
- Timeline

Example:

> Will you be able to help me put together some slides on O.R. complication rates for the last calendar year? Let me know if you have time.
>
> Thanks.

This email is missing a lot of the points we listed above, assuming that the recipient is receiving this with minimal context. A reasonable reader would ask for more details. If we can expect a reader would want those details, we should just give them from the start. If we apply some of the concepts above, your request becomes clear and the recipient doesn't need to get those details from you, and potentially follow-up with you multiple times.

I will need your help putting together a presentation Friday of next week. I am going to present to the C-suite regarding O.R. complications.

I would appreciate if you could compile the O.R. complication rates:

- from the last calendar year
- by specialty
- by individual surgeon

The raw numbers would be fine, but if you can put them on slides that I can plug into the rest of my presentation, that would be ideal.

I would need this by next *Wednesday at the latest.*

Let me know if you can help.

Thanks.

The request in the second version is more clear. The reader has a lot of the information they need in order to start seeing not only if they can help, but also has enough information to get started on the project. There is now less need for back and forth communication and expectations are clear.

Example:

Thanks for setting up the time last week for the demonstration of your company's capabilities.

After discussion with our leadership team, we have chosen your company as our vendor. I think with your company's help, we will make marked improvements in our lab turnaround times and capacity. Let's discuss next steps.

A reasonable reader will likely want to know what the next steps are so that they know what to expect and what to prepare for. Spell out the next steps, even if it is just in general terms.

Thanks for setting up the time last week for the demonstration of your company's capabilities.

After discussion with our leadership team, we have chosen your company as our vendor. I think with your company's help, we will make marked improvements in our lab turnaround times and capacity.
As some next steps:

- Please send me a copy of your company's contract, so that our legal department and leadership team can review it in detail. They will reach out to you directly if they have any questions.
- Our leadership has already ok'ed me to put you in contact with the heads of the lab and materials management division so that you can begin to preliminarily coordinate with them. I will introduce them to you in a separate email. Please keep me cc'ed on communications with them.

In the second version, the reader knows what to expect as far as next steps as they were specifically stated.

Use the Subject Line to Express the Main Takeaway Point of Your Email

Using the subject line to deliver the main takeaway point is an application of the concept of leading with your conclusion. When you do this, your readers will be able to understand the body your email in light of your subject. Using the subject as a title will also enable them to prioritize your email better.

You will not be able to do this with every email. However, when you are able to do it, it is an effective tool to improve the understanding of the whole email.

Example:

Update to ICU protocol

This could describe a wide variety of changes. With some more specificity, your readers will know what to expect within the email. They be able to judge its importance, and will understand the context of the body of the email better. A good way to do this is to provide the gist of the update.

ICU protocol update: call pharmacist for every cardiac arrest

This simple statement gives an anchoring point that helps your readers understand the contents of the email.

Example:

Interesting article

This could be virtually anything. Some specificity lets the reader know what to expect, and as above, lets them judge its importance to them.

Our clinic's new patient retention program gets positive press

This second version lets the readers know exactly what kind of article to expect, potentially heightening the impact of the email and the article it references.

Beware of The Use of Reply All

A frequent email error I see from medical professionals is the inappropriate use of Reply All.

Reply All sends your message to *every, single recipient* on the recipient list. If there are 1,000 people on the list, you will send an email to all 1,000 of them. That's fine if that's your intent. However, if that is not your intent, then select exactly who you want to contact and send your message only to them.

When replying to a mass email, take an extra moment, ask yourself who you want to receive your message, and make sure you are hitting the right button.

Tone

The quickness and frequency of emails in business communications makes it easy to forget our tone with emails. To minimize the chance of your emails being misunderstood, before you send the email, take a moment to:

- Proofread the email
- Consider the point-of-view of the person reading
- Ask yourself, "In what ways can the reader(s) misinterpret this email?"

CC

"CC" stands for "carbon copy". This references an old method of making duplicate paperwork.

You should be CC'ing or copying people who are interested parties. These recipients are not the main recipient of the email. In this way, you inform parties that are interested but not necessarily direct participants. Think of CC'ed people as spectators. They're not expected to chime in. However, they may chime in if they have something important to add.

For example, if your director instructed you to coordinate on a project with the head of public relations and you think it's important for your director to see the progress with each email, CC your director in your emails with the head of public relations pertaining to that project.

BCC

BCC is "blind carbon copy". People on this list will be invisible to others on the email. This is essentially letting them eavesdrop on the email conversation. Use BCC if you want to inform someone of an email, but do not want others to know. However, the BCC'ed person can Reply All and the whole group will know.

Use BCC only in very unusual circumstances.

Email chains

Email chains happen when there is a series of sequential replies to the original email. In an email chain you reply to a reply to a reply, and so on. The result is a record of written conversation.

Sometimes the topic changes and the conversation continues. In those cases, it can be better to start a new email chain for that new topic. Mixing multiple topics in email chains makes searching for relevant conversations later on more difficult.

Slide Presentation Basics

Slide presentations are common tools in business.

When done properly, slides are effective tools to communicate with both a live audience and an audience who cannot be present in real time.

When done poorly, slides confuse, frustrate, and disengage an audience. In these cases, they leave a bad impression.

The general concepts and tools in earlier sections will apply here:

- Write with your audience in mind
- Write short, simple sentences
- Use concrete details
- Lead with your conclusion

2 general styles of slide presentations:

1. Notes to yourself to guide you through your presentation materials
2. Resources for your audience to review later

1. Notes to Yourself

When you make notes to yourself, put minimal text on each slide. The text serves to remind you what to talk about. It also serves to anchor your audience's attention on the central concept or theme that you are talking about. A simple, compelling visual can also serve the same purpose as minimal text. In these cases, the slides are of little use to those who have not been in the audience when you gave your presentation. The key here is that **the presentation itself is a supplement to you.**

2. Resources for Your Audience to Review Later

By contrast, making your presentation a resource for your audience to review later is the opposite of making the presentation notes to yourself. In this case, **you act as a supplement for the presentation**. You fill in gaps, make connections, and add color commentary. However, the slides can speak for themselves, and do not need you.

Beware of a common trap in giving these kinds of presentations. A big mistake is to start reading off of the slides robotically, without filling in the gaps, making connections, or adding color commentary.

The following examples are for a presentation regarding antibiotic use based on an older guideline that could be given to either fellow healthcare professionals or to a nonclinical audience.

Example: Notes to yourself

ANTIBIOTIC COVERAGE FOR HOSPITAL-ACQUIRED PNEUMONIA

S. Aureus

P. Aeruginosa/gram-negative bacilli

Example: Resource for your audience

ANTIBIOTIC COVERAGE FOR HOSPITAL-ACQUIRED PNEUMONIA

Empiric coverage IDSA 2016 recommendations :

- **S. aureus**
  - Suspected MRSA → vancomycin or linezolid
  - Suspected MSSA → oxacillin, nafcillin, or cefazolin
- **P. aeruginosa** and other gram-negative bacilli
  - Suspected. P. aeruginosa → Antibiotics from 2 different classes with anti- *P. aeruginosa* activity
  - No suspected. P. aeruginosa → Single antibiotic with anti-*P. aeruginosa* activity
  - No aminoglycoside monotherapy

If You Title Your Slides, Make Your Titles Headlines

Like a headline, if you use slide titles, make the key takeaway the title, doing this will center your audience around the point that you're trying to make. It will also encourage you to make each point in the slide support the title.

When you make your titles headlines, try to make your series of headlines read like a cohesive story. If you do this right, someone doing a quick readthrough will understand the main points of your presentation and how they fit together from the slide titles alone.

Example: generic title

ANTIBIOTIC COVERAGE FOR HOSPITAL-ACQUIRED PNEUMONIA

Empiric coverage IDSA 2016 recommendations :
- **S. aureus**
  - Suspected MRSA → vancomycin or linezolid
  - Suspected MSSA → oxacillin, nafcillin, or cefazolin

- **P. aeruginosa** and other gram-negative bacilli
  - Suspected. P. aeruginosa → Antibiotics from 2 different classes with anti- *P. aeruginosa* activity
  - No suspected. P. aeruginosa → Single antibiotic with anti-*P. aeruginosa* activity
  - No aminoglycoside monotherapy

Example: Making the title the key takeaway

HOSPITAL-ACQUIRED PNEUMONIA REQUIRES BROAD ANTIBIOTIC COVERAGE

Empiric coverage IDSA 2016 recommendations:

- **S. aureus**
  - Suspected MRSA → vancomycin or linezolid
  - Suspected MSSA → oxacillin, nafcillin, or cefazolin

- **P. aeruginosa** and other gram-negative bacilli
  - Suspected. P. aeruginosa →Antibiotics from 2 different classes with anti- *P. aeruginosa* activity
  - No suspected. P. aeruginosa → Single antibiotic with anti-*P. aeruginosa* activity
  - No aminoglycoside monotherapy

Make only a handful of points per slide

Slides get cluttered very quickly. As much as possible, keep your slides to a handful of points at most. Over-cluttering your slides makes them harder to read. This holds true whether you're using images, text, or a combination of both.

Sometimes you'll have to make one slide into 2 or more slides.

Example: more cluttered

HOSPITAL-ACQUIRED PNEUMONIA REQUIRES BOTH MRSA AND PSEUDOMONAS COVERAGE

Empiric coverage IDSA 2016 recommendations:

- **S. aureus**
  - Suspected MRSA → vancomycin or linezolid
  - Suspected MSSA → oxacillin, nafcillin, or cefazolin

- **P. aeruginosa** and other gram-negative bacilli
  - Suspected. P. aeruginosa → Antibiotics from 2 different classes with anti- *P. aeruginosa* activity
  - No suspected. P. aeruginosa → Single antibiotic with anti-*P. aeruginosa* activity
  - No aminoglycoside monotherapy

Example: less cluttered and separated over 2 slides

HOSPITAL-ACQUIRED PNEUMONIA REQUIRES BOTH MRSA AND PSEUDOMONAS COVERAGE

Empiric coverage IDSA 2016 recommendations:
- **S. aureus**
  - Suspected MRSA → vancomycin or linezolid
  - Suspected MSSA → oxacillin, nafcillin, or cefazolin

HOSPITAL-ACQUIRED PNEUMONIA REQUIRES BOTH MRSA AND PSEUDOMONAS COVERAGE

Empiric coverage IDSA 2016 recommendations:
- **P. aeruginosa** and other gram-negative bacilli
  - Suspected. P. aeruginosa → Antibiotics from 2 different classes with anti- *P. aeruginosa* activity
  - No suspected. P. aeruginosa → Single antibiotic with anti- *P. aeruginosa* activity
  - No aminoglycoside monotherapy

<u>Use Formatting to Your Advantage</u>

When presenting content, ask yourself whether it's better represented in a single text box vs columns, rows, or combination of these. The ability to re-arrange the format of a slide, in a way that meets your needs, is an under-appreciated aspect of using slides to make a presentation.

Example: single text box

HOSPITAL-ACQUIRED PNEUMONIA REQUIRES BROAD ANTIBIOTIC COVERAGE

Empiric coverage IDSA 2016 recommendations:

· **S. aureus**
  · Suspected MRSA → vancomycin or linezolid
  · Suspected MSSA → oxacillin, nafcillin, or cefazolin

· **P. aeruginosa** and other gram-negative bacilli
  · Suspected. P. aeruginosa →Antibiotics from 2 different classes with anti- *P. aeruginosa* activity
  · No suspected. P. aeruginosa → Single antibiotic with anti-*P. aeruginosa* activity
  · No aminoglycoside monotherapy

Example: 2 columns

HOSPITAL-ACQUIRED PNEUMONIA REQUIRES BROAD ANTIBIOTIC COVERAGE

Empiric coverage IDSA 2016 recommendations:

- **S. aureus**
  - Suspected MRSA
    - vancomycin or linezolid
  - Suspected MSSA
    - oxacillin, nafcillin, or cefazolin

- **P. aeruginosa** and other gram-negative bacilli
  - Suspected. P. aeruginosa
    - Antibiotics from 2 different classes with anti- *P. aeruginosa* activity
  - No suspected. P. aeruginosa
    - Single antibiotic with anti-*P. aeruginosa* activity
  - No aminoglycoside monotherapy

Example: 2 columns and a callout box

HOSPITAL-ACQUIRED PNEUMONIA REQUIRES BROAD ANTIBIOTIC COVERAGE

Empiric coverage IDSA 2016 recommendations:

- **S. aureus**
  - Suspected MRSA
    - vancomycin or linezolid
  - Suspected MSSA
    - oxacillin, nafcillin, or cefazolin

- **P. aeruginosa** and other gram-negative bacilli
  - Suspected. P. aeruginosa
    - Antibiotics from 2 different classes with anti- *P. aeruginosa* activity
  - No suspected. P. aeruginosa
    - Single antibiotic with anti-*P. aeruginosa* activity

No aminoglycoside monotherapy for gram negative coverage

Highlight important, secondary points

When there are secondary points that you want to highlight in addition to the main point of your title — consider using a colored box, or highlighting the text.

Example: simple highlighting

HOSPITAL-ACQUIRED PNEUMONIA REQUIRES BROAD ANTIBIOTIC COVERAGE

Empiric coverage IDSA 2016 recommendations:

- **S. aureus**
  - Suspected MRSA → vancomycin or linezolid
  - Suspected MSSA → oxacillin, nafcillin, or cefazolin

- **P. aeruginosa** and other gram-negative bacilli
  - Suspected. P. aeruginosa →Antibiotics from 2 different classes with anti- *P. aeruginosa* activity
  - No suspected. P. aeruginosa → Single antibiotic with anti-*P. aeruginosa* activity
  - No aminoglycoside monotherapy

Example: colored box (looks similar to highlighting)

HOSPITAL-ACQUIRED PNEUMONIA REQUIRES BROAD ANTIBIOTIC COVERAGE

Empiric coverage IDSA 2016 recommendations:

- **S. aureus**
  - Suspected MRSA →vancomycin or linezolid
  - Suspected MSSA → oxacillin, nafcillin, or cefazolin

- **P. aeruginosa** and other gram-negative bacilli
  - Suspected. P. aeruginosa →Antibiotics from 2 different classes with anti- *P. aeruginosa* activity
  - No suspected. P. aeruginosa → Single antibiotic with anti-*P. aeruginosa* activity
  - No aminoglycoside monotherapy

Example: colored box for a callout

HOSPITAL-ACQUIRED PNEUMONIA REQUIRES BROAD ANTIBIOTIC COVERAGE

Empiric coverage IDSA 2016 recommendations:

- **S. aureus**
  - Suspected MRSA
    - vancomycin or linezolid
  - Suspected MSSA
    - oxacillin, nafcillin, or cefazolin

- **P. aeruginosa** and other gram-negative bacilli
  - Suspected. P. aeruginosa
    - Antibiotics from 2 different classes with anti- *P. aeruginosa* activity
  - No suspected. P. aeruginosa
    - Single antibiotic with anti-*P. aeruginosa* activity

No aminoglycoside monotherapy for gram negative coverage

<u>Use colored shapes</u>

Consider using colored shapes to differentiate ideas. The colored shapes serve to differentiate concepts or facts.

Example: Without colored shapes

ANTIBIOTIC COVERAGE FOR HOSPITAL-ACQUIRED PNEUMONIA

<u>S. Aureus</u>

<u>P. Aeruginosa/gram-negative bacilli</u>

Example: With colored shapes and format change

ANTIBIOTIC COVERAGE FOR HOSPITAL-ACQUIRED PNEUMONIA

<u>S. Aureus</u>

<u>P. Aeruginosa/gram-negative bacilli</u>

Example: Colored shapes with additional detail

ANTIBIOTIC COVERAGE FOR HOSPITAL-ACQUIRED PNEUMONIA

Empiric coverage IDSA 2016 recommendations :

S. aureus
- Suspected MRSA → vancomycin or linezolid
- Suspected MSSA → oxacillin, nafcillin, or cefazolin

P. aeruginosa and other gram-negative bacilli
- Suspected. P. aeruginosa →Antibiotics from 2 different classes with anti- *P. aeruginosa* activity
- No suspected. P. aeruginosa → Single antibiotic with anti-*P. aeruginosa* activity
- No aminoglycoside monotherapy

Use Easy-to-Follow Flowcharts

Often, a simple but well-done flowchart can communicate the same information as volumes of text. However, flowcharts can become overcluttered. As much as possible, keep them simple and easy to follow at a glance.

Like images, use flowcharts with care and be selective in using them.

Example: Flowchart

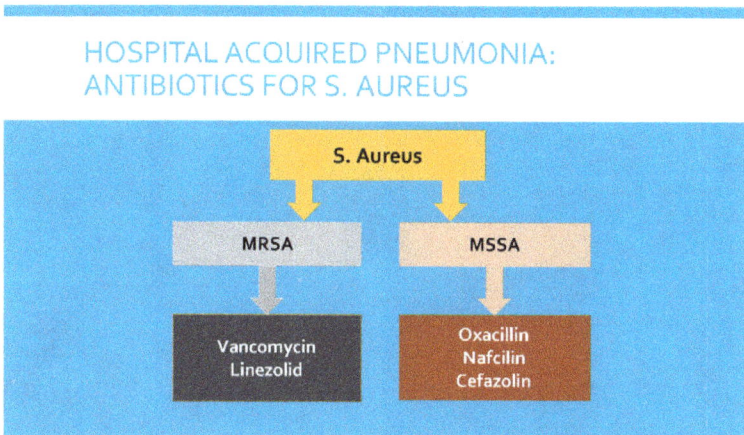

HOSPITAL ACQUIRED PNEUMONIA: ANTIBIOTICS FOR S. AUREUS

S. Aureus

MRSA → Vancomycin, Linezolid

MSSA → Oxacillin, Nafcilin, Cefazolin

Use Images That Are Clear and Simple.

Images are useful tools in a presentation. Often, they are more powerful than text alone. However, just like over-cluttering with words, you can over-clutter your slide with too many images, or images that are too busy. Choose images that are easy to understand at a glance.

Choose your images with care and be selective in using them.

Use Media Assets Such as Videos Sparingly

If you use features such as sound, video, or animations, use them with a clear purpose. They're powerful tools. However, like any tool, there's a time and a place for them. Using them in the wrong time and place can cause distraction, making your presentation less effective.

Overusing these features weakens their impact as well. When you're thinking about using these features in your presentation, ask yourself if it will increase or decrease your presentation's effectiveness.

Final Thoughts

I hope that this book has opened your eyes to some tools for written communication and how to apply them to business-oriented communications.

The best way to further your understanding of business writing is by doing it. It's a skill that takes time, practice, and persistent effort. But the more you do it, the easier it becomes.

Business writing is a skill worth investing in as you expand your healthcare career whether it's in a clinical setting or business one. Writing well will help you capitalize on opportunities. It will help convince people of your value as a professional.

I encourage anyone interested in sharpening their writing skills beyond the fundamentals discussed in this book to seek out resources for more advanced writing skills. You will find it worth your time and energy.

Good luck!

Additional Resources

Below are suggestions for additional resources that can help you advance your skills in specific aspects of business writing.

Guides to Better Writing

The Elements of Style

by William Strunk and E.B. White

How to Write a Sentence: And How to Read One

By Stanley Fish

On Writing: A Memoir of The Craft

By Stephen King

Guides to Better Slide Presentations

The Visual Slide Revolution

By Dave Paradi

slide:ology: The Art and Science of Creating Great Presentations

By Nancy Duarte

Acknowledgements

Special thanks to the following people who helped me with this book at its many stages of development:

Brendon Blake

Antonio Mendez, MD, JD

Tanya Pohl, JD

www.ingramcontent.com/pod-product-compliance
Lightning Source LLC
Chambersburg PA
CBHW071749200326
41519CB00021BC/6924